WIDE RANGE
SCIENCE STORIES 1

Michael Holt and
Alan Ward

Oliver & Boyd

Illustrated by Michael Whittlesea
Cover illustration by Gordon King

Oliver & Boyd
Robert Stevenson House
1–3 Baxter's Place
Leith Walk
Edinburgh EH1 3BB
A Division of Longman Group Ltd

ISBN 0 05 003290 9

First published 1982
Second impression 1982

Printed in Hong Kong by
Sheck Wah Tong Printing Press Ltd.

Preface

This series is an attempt to introduce junior school children to important ideas and experiences in science through the medium of stories. It is not in any way a science course, but we hope that it may be helpful in expanding the range and content of children's reading and introducing them to the world of science. The stories have all been chosen to relate to the kind of ideas the intended young reader finds comprehensible and interesting.

The four books of the series are written for children of reading ages 7 + to 11 +. Book One is broadly suitable for children of reading age 7 + to 8 +, Book Two for 8 + to 9 +, Book Three for 9 + to 10 + and Book Four for 10 + to 11 +.

Contents

Animals We Shall Never See Again

Nowadays many people are worried
because we are killing so many wild animals.
If we do not stop, we may never see
some wild animals again.
They will become extinct.
Animals that are extinct have died out.
No one will ever see them again.

● ● ● ● ● ●

There are now very few tigers
living in the wild.
This is because tigers have been hunted
for hundreds of years.

Their fur is very beautiful
and some people hunt them for this.
Other people hunt them for sport.
An Indian prince once boasted
that he had shot two thousand tigers!

If people go on killing tigers
there will soon be none left.

There are many other animals in danger,
and there are some that are already extinct.
In the last three hundred years
many types of animals have died out.
They have become extinct
because they have been hunted to death.

●　●　●　●　●　●

Here are stories of two birds
that we shall never see again.

The first of these is the dodo,
which is the best known
of all the extinct birds.

Dodos used to live on two small islands
in the Indian Ocean.
Nobody lived on these islands,

but more than three hundred years ago
a ship from Portugal stopped there.
Some of the sailors landed on the island
to see if they could find food.

While they were looking for food
they saw some large birds.
These birds were nearly one metre tall
and they weighed about twenty-five kilograms.
They were as big as turkeys
and they strutted about in the same way.

The birds were not afraid of people
and the sailors caught them easily.
They called them by a word
which meant "silly" in their language,
and we still use that word
when we call them dodos.

The dodos had lived in peace
on their small islands
for thousands of years.
There were no enemies to fear
and, perhaps because of this,
they could not fly.
They still had short little wings

but they had lost the power of flight.
This made them very easy to catch
and the sailors killed them at once.

Other sailors from other ships
did the same.   They liked the taste
of roast dodo.

A Dutchman from another ship
caught a dodo alive and took it
back with him to Holland.
When the people there
saw the captured dodo
they were very interested.
They wondered about it
and they talked about it.
Artists made paintings of it,
like the one shown opposite.

Only a few years after the sailors
first saw the dodos,
all these gentle birds were dead.
The sailors killed them for food,
but that was not the only harm they did.
They also left cats, dogs and pigs
on the islands.

These animals did not attack the dodos,
but they did eat their eggs.
So every year fewer and fewer dodo chicks
hatched out.

Every year more dodos were killed.
In the end there were no dodos
left on the islands at all.
The last one died in 1681.

Another bird that became extinct
more than a hundred years ago
was the great auk.
Great auks lived on islands
in the cold seas around Europe,
and in North America.
They looked very like the puffins
which still live in these cold seas.
   Many of the great auks lived on
Penguin Island, which was
in the Baltic Sea.
But one day in 1830 the sea-bed shifted.

Penguin Island sank under the sea.
Nearly all the great auks drowned
and only a few reached the nearby island
of Eldey.   Eldey has very steep cliffs
and there was only one spot
where the auks could climb out of the sea.

Only a few of the auks that had
swum to Eldey found the one place
where they could climb out of the water.
These lucky ones settled down on Eldey.
Here they laid eggs
and brought up their young.
They could live in peace
because there were no people on Eldey Island.

Once there had been great auks in America
as well, but they had all been killed.
Men had hunted them for their skins,
which were worth a lot of money.
Not only were the birds killed for their skins
but their eggs were taken too,
because they were good to eat.
Taking their eggs killed the auks
far faster than simply hunting them.

In the end the hunters said,
   "All the auks must be dead.
There are no more to catch."
So people offered even more money
for the skin of a great auk.
   Then a fisherman from the
cold northern seas
remembered that auks used to live
on Eldey Island.
He thought that perhaps they
still lived there.
So, one night in 1844
he sailed in a small boat
from Iceland to Eldey.
He sailed with some friends,
who were also fishermen,
and they sailed all through the night.
Next morning the fishermen saw Eldey.
Two of them went ashore
at the one place on the island
where they could land.
They climbed on to the island
to start their search for great auks.

They did not have to look very hard.
Only two great auks were left on the island.
They were the last two great auks
in the world.
They walked tamely up to the two men,
who killed them at once.
The poor birds had not tried to escape
because they were not afraid of people.
If they had been afraid,
there might still be great auks alive today.

The fishermen took the birds
and sailed back to Iceland.
There they sold the two skins.
   Those two great auks had been
the last two in the world.
Now they were dead
and these birds were extinct.

●　　●　　●　　●　　●　　●

The dodo and the great auk
are only two of the many animals
killed off by people.
Other animals are still in danger.
We must save these animals.
If we do not help to save them
and their way of life,
we shall never see them again.

Saving the River Thames

The biggest river in England
is the River Thames.
It flows through the capital city, London.

Two hundred years ago the River Thames
was well-known as a salmon river.
Each year the London fishermen caught
more than three thousand salmon
in the Thames, and they sold these fish
in the London markets.

Salmon were not the only fish
in the Thames.
The river was rich in smelts, shad,
flounders, whitebait and lampreys.
Every day some thirty or forty boats
went out with their nets
and brought back large catches.

The fishermen caught as many as
fifty thousand smelts in a single day,
and up to a million lampreys every year.
In those days it was not always easy to get
fresh meat, so fresh fish from the Thames
helped to keep the people of London
happy and healthy.

Then about two hundred years ago,
the fish in the River Thames began to die.
They died because the river had become
too dirty for them to live in.
As London grew larger
the river became more and more polluted.
More and more people poured their sewage
into the Thames.

More and more factories
tipped their waste straight into
the slow-moving river.
Each year more and more fish died,
and by 1920 there were no fish in
the Thames at London.
The river itself was dead.
Not only was it dead
but it also smelt terrible.
On hot days the smell was like
thousands of rotting eggs.
The people of London were horrified.

"We must clean the Thames," they said.
"London is a capital city and we want
to be proud of our river."

They decided that they would clean
the Thames and they hoped that one day
fish would be able to live in
the river again.

It took more than twenty years
to clean the river
and it cost millions of pounds.
Nowadays all the sewage is cleaned
before it goes into the river.
Factories may not tip their waste
straight into the water.
Scientists test the water all the time
to make sure that it is pure.

Now there are fish in the river again.
In 1974 a salmon was caught
in the Thames.
This was the first one since June, 1833.

•   •   •   •   •   •

Today London can be proud of its river.
The Thames is cleaner than any other river
flowing through a capital city.
There are still many dirty rivers in Britain,
but London has shown that dirty rivers
can be cleaned.

Edward Jenner

For hundreds of years everyone in the world
was frightened of catching smallpox.
Every year thousands of people
died of this disease.

When people catch smallpox
nasty blisters appear all over their bodies.
They have a fever and a very high
temperature.   They may get well again,
but the blisters leave nasty scars behind
on their faces and bodies.

Some diseases, like smallpox, measles
and chickenpox, are caused by germs.
Germs are like very tiny animals.
They are so small that you can only see them
with a microscope.
If germs get into your body
they can give you a disease.
Cold germs can give you a cold,
smallpox germs can give you smallpox.
These germs come from someone
who has the disease.

Smallpox is very dangerous,
much more dangerous than a cold.
Doctors cannot cure it,
but they can make sure
that you don't catch it.

Today very few people catch smallpox.
Only one or two people catch it each year
in the whole of the world.
This is because of one doctor and
what he discovered about smallpox germs.

•　　•　　•　　•　　•　　•

This doctor was Edward Jenner.
He was an English country doctor
who lived
about two hundred
years ago.

He worked in a little village
called Berkeley, in Gloucestershire.
In those days,
smallpox was still a common disease.
Dr Jenner often wondered
if there was anything he could do
to stop people catching it.
He wanted to prevent smallpox.

Most of Dr Jenner's patients were farmers
or worked on farms.
These men and women
often talked to Edward Jenner
about smallpox.
They said that if you caught cowpox
you would never catch smallpox.
Cowpox is a mild form of smallpox.
Both people and cattle get it,
but you do not die of cowpox.
You only get sores on your hands
like little blisters.

Edward Jenner also knew
that if you caught smallpox — and lived! —
you never caught it again.

Jenner began to think
about these two diseases.

In those days some people thought
that the Devil brought diseases.
So there was nothing to do but pray to God.
Jenner did not believe this.
He thought that diseases were caused
by germs, which came from other people.
He had an idea that if your body
could fight the germs and kill them,
then you would not catch the disease.
He thought that cowpox germs
might help the body to fight
smallpox germs.

Edward Jenner did not know that
his idea was the beginning
of a completely new kind of medicine.
It was the beginning of a new way
of preventing disease.
But Dr Jenner did know that he must prove
that his idea was right.
He knew that he would have to
find out more about cowpox germs

and smallpox germs.
He had to make an experiment
to show if his idea was right or wrong.

A chance to make his experiment
came in 1796, on the 14th of May.
A young milkmaid came to see him
with sores on her hands.
Her name was Sarah Nelmes and
she milked cows on a nearby farm.
Dr Jenner looked carefully at her hands.
They were covered with little red sores
that looked like blisters.
Dr Jenner knew what was the matter with her.

"You have caught cowpox from the cows,"
he said. He squeezed the sores gently
and some liquid oozed out.
He put this liquid from her sores
into a small bottle,
because he needed it for his experiment.
Then he looked after her carefully
until she got better.

Dr Jenner also took some liquid
from the sores of a patient
with mild smallpox.
He stored this in another bottle.

Now he was ready to start his experiment.
First he would give someone cowpox.
To do this, he would use the cowpox liquid
that he had taken from Sarah's sores.
When the cowpox was over,
he would try to give
the same person smallpox.
To do this he would use the smallpox liquid.
Dr Jenner thought to himself:

"The cowpox germs will make the body
able to defend itself

against the dangerous smallpox germs.
My patient will not catch smallpox."
If his experiment worked,
Dr Jenner would have found a way
of preventing smallpox.
If his experiment failed
and his patient died,
Dr Jenner would be a murderer.
So you see that it was
a very dangerous experiment to make.

Dr Jenner went to see a local farmer
called Mr Phipps.
Mr Phipps had an eight-year-old son, James.
Dr Jenner told Mr Phipps what he wanted.
"I want to use your son
to test my idea about smallpox.
If I am right, he will never catch smallpox.
I know it is dangerous,
but I am sure it will work."
Surprisingly, Mr Phipps agreed.
"You can make your experiment on James,"
he said.   Mr Phipps took a chair outside
his house.

James sat on a cushion
to make himself higher.
A servant held James firmly
while farmer Phipps looked on from the door.
Dr Jenner made two small cuts
in James's left arm.
Into the cuts he put some liquid
from Sarah's cowpox sores.
Then he bandaged James's arm
and sent him to bed.
Dr Jenner told Mr Phipps,
    "James will catch cowpox in a few days,
but he won't be very ill."

Mr and Mrs Phipps waited
to see what would happen.
Sure enough, as Dr Jenner said,
James caught cowpox.
But he was not very ill
and in six weeks' time
he was perfectly well again.

Now Dr Jenner was ready
to do the second part of the experiment.
This was the dangerous part.
This time he was going to use
the smallpox liquid.
Dr Jenner went to see James again.
He made a cut in James's arm
and put in the smallpox liquid.

"There you are!" said Dr Jenner.
Then he spoke to Mr Phipps,
"Now we will have to wait and see.
I hope that James won't catch smallpox,
but we must wait two weeks
before we can be sure.
Don't you worry.
I will come and see him every day."

The next day and every day after that
Dr Jenner came to visit James.
Each day he asked,
   "How are you feeling, James?"
Each day James answered,
   "I feel well, thank you, Doctor."
Each day Dr Jenner looked to see
if James had got any sores.

After two weeks he still had no sores
on his face or body.
He had not caught smallpox!
   Dr Jenner's experiment had worked!
He had found a way to stop
the smallpox germs.

Now he needed a name for what he had done.
He had used *cow*pox germs to fight smallpox,
so he used the Latin word *vacca*,
which means *a cow*.
He called his idea vaccination.
He had vaccinated James against smallpox.

Then Dr Jenner went to London
to tell doctors there about vaccination.
They laughed at him.
They all thought he was a fool.
Someone drew a cartoon
of people who had been vaccinated.
There are cows' heads
bursting out all over them.

Though people laughed at him,
Dr Jenner kept on with his work.
Soon some doctors believed him.
They found that vaccination worked.
It really did prevent smallpox.

By 1800, only four years
after he had vaccinated James,
most doctors in England
were using his ideas.
Parliament gave Jenner £30 000
so that he could go on making tests.

•   •   •   •   •   •

Dr Jenner's work
began a war against smallpox.
Today this war is won,
but it has taken a very long time.

Dr Jenner started his work on vaccination
nearly two hundred years ago.
During all that time
people have been catching smallpox.
Today people are vaccinated
if there is any danger from smallpox.
Very few people ever catch it.

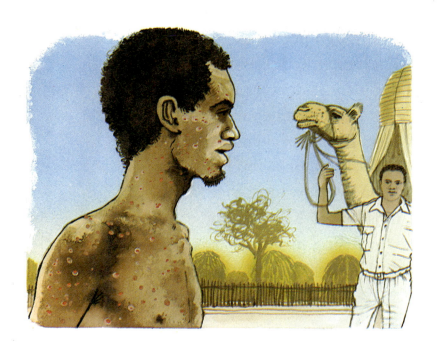

In 1977 a man died of smallpox in Africa,
and in 1978 a woman in Britain died.
But in 1979 and 1980 there were no deaths
from smallpox anywhere in the world.
In the picture on this page
you can see Ali Maalin, from Somalia.
He caught smallpox, but he recovered.
Doctors think he is the last man in
the world to have had the disease.
Scientists are sure now

that the war against smallpox is won.

•　　•　　•　　•　　•　　•

Edward Jenner died many years ago,
but we still remember him.
He was a very brave man.
We remember James Phipps too,
because he helped Dr Jenner
to do his first experiment.
James was also very brave.
Without him, Dr Jenner
could not have made his test.
Without that first vaccination
he could not have stopped smallpox.

Birds on the Wing

This story is about birds
which spend part of the year in Britain
and part of the year in other countries.
Each year these birds fly
thousands of kilometres over land and sea,
with only the sun to guide them.

They do this to find their food.
During the winter in Britain
some birds cannot find the food
they need.   They have to fly away
to a country where it is warmer.

Swallows do this every year.
At the end of summer,
in August or September,
they gather in huge flocks.
Have you seen them sitting
on telephone wires and
on the branches of trees?

From Britain they fly to South Africa,
where it is sunny and warm.
In South Africa they can find the insects
that they eat.   In March or April
the swallows fly back to Britain.
These long, long journeys
are called migrations.

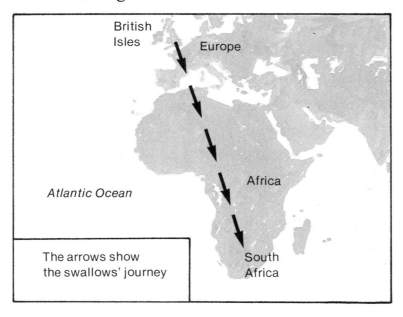

British
Isles
Europe

Atlantic Ocean

Africa

The arrows show
the swallows' journey

South
Africa

Swallows migrate every year.
They travel in flocks of
several thousand birds,
all flying in the same direction.

The journey of more than
eight thousand kilometres
takes them between six and eight weeks.
They fly during the day and
at night they sleep in branches of trees
or in beds of reeds by the side of
lakes and rivers.

Different kinds of birds
migrate to different places.
Swallows from Russia and Poland
fly to central Africa every winter,
and back to Russia and Poland in the summer.

● ● ● ● ● ●

Some birds fly to Britain
for the winter.   Many geese and ducks
come from the cold lands of the North
to spend the winter in Britain.
Their own countries are covered
in deep snow and all the rivers and lakes
are frozen.   The birds have nowhere
to swim or look for food.

Some of the birds which do this are:

barnacle geese
ducks
sea birds

Iceland
redwing

and some song birds such as:

Iceland redwings

Barnacle goose

Lapland
bunting

Lapland buntings
snow buntings.

All these birds come to Britain
every autumn in October or November.
They are not easy to see because
they are wild birds
and easily scared by humans.
Perhaps you will see one
when you walk in the countryside,
if you are very quiet.

Duck

These birds stay in Britain
for four or five months
before flying north again in spring.
Most of them fly back in March or April,
but sometimes, if the winter has been mild,
they fly back in February.

All these birds fly thousands of kilometres
between one country and another.
How do they find their way?
How do they know which way to fly
over the wide oceans and great deserts?
They have no maps to help them
on their long journeys.

Scientists have tried to discover
how migrating birds find their way.

Some birds use the sun to guide them.
They fly along a line that keeps
the same angle to the sun.
They can do this
even though the sun is moving all the time.

Some birds, such as hedge sparrows
and lesser whitethroats, fly by night.
They find their way by the moon
and by the stars.

•   •   •   •   •   •

How do birds know when it is time
to fly away for the winter?
Scientists are not sure,
but they have found out some things.

Some birds have a sort of clock
inside their bodies.
It is not a real clock.
It is like the clock inside you
that tells your milk teeth
when it is time to fall out.
The bird's clock tells it
when it is time to fly away for the winter.

•　　•　　•　　•　　•　　•

How do we know all this
about migrating birds?
How do we know that swallows
really go to southern Africa?

For many, many years people in Britain
knew that something happened
to swallows in the winter.
In the summer there were swallows
in every town and village.

Then suddenly, when autumn began,
they were gone.   What had happened to them?
Some people were sure that
the swallows had flown away.
But where to?   Nobody knew.
Other people said,
    "No, the swallows are still here.
But they are hiding.
They have all gone to sleep
for the winter and next spring
they will wake up again."
These people thought that swallows
were like hedgehogs and tortoises
which sleep during the winter.
They thought the swallows slept
in the mud at the bottom of ponds.
    Who was right?   Did the swallows
fly away, or were they asleep
in hidden nests?   How could people find out?
They found out just as people find out now.
They watched and they did experiments.
    Nowadays people who are interested in birds
find out like this.

They catch birds in nets or traps.
Then they put rings round their legs.
It does not hurt the bird at all.
The metal ring has a number on it
and an address.
Then the birds are set free.

    Bird watchers in other countries
look out for birds with rings on their legs.
If they find one, they read the number
and address on the ring.
They write to the address
saying what the number was on the ring
and where they found the bird.

Thousands of bird watchers do this every year. Scientists read all their letters and work out how many birds have migrated, and where they migrate to.

That is how we know which bird flies the longest distance during its migration. It is the Arctic tern. It flies from Greenland all the way to the Antarctic.

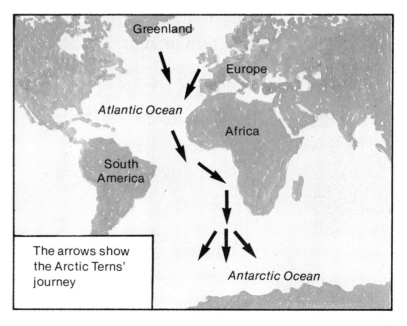

Greenland

Europe

Atlantic Ocean

Africa

South America

The arrows show the Arctic Terns' journey

Antarctic Ocean

This is a journey of about
fourteen thousand kilometres
and it takes the birds about five months.
In that time they fly
almost halfway round the world.
They have to fly all the time.
They even have to sleep as they fly.
But we still don't know
how they manage to find their way.

Perhaps when you grow up
you may find the answer.

Making a Bird Table

In winter, many birds
find it difficult to get enough food.
You can help by giving them food and water.
The best way to do this
is by building a bird table.

● ● ● ● ● ●

Make your table out of a wooden board.
A good size is about thirty centimetres square.
Bore four holes in the board,
one at each corner.
Then nail some wood strips
round the sides of the board.
The birds will perch on these.
Cut two lengths of strong string
about one metre long.
Thread these through the holes in the board.

If there is a tree with a low branch
(about one and a half metres off the ground)
near your school or home,
you can hang your bird table there.
If not, you can make a wall support like this.
Don't forget –
your table must be
out of reach of cats.

On the table put a plastic dish of water,
and food for the birds.
Here are some of the things to put
on your table:
seeds (from pet shops or collected from plants)
peanuts
breadcrumbs (brown or white)
cold boiled potato
apple cores
pieces of bacon rind
bits of fat or suet

Not all birds eat the same foods.
Make a list of the birds you see
at your table.   See if you can work out
which birds like which foods.

Important
There are two things you must remember
if you make a bird table.
1 Feed the birds only in winter.
   In summer they need water,
   but not your food.
2 If you start feeding birds in winter,
   do not stop until warm weather returns.

"Catseyes" Percy Shaw

If you have driven in a car by night,
you will have seen a line of lights
along the middle of the road.
We call them catseyes.

They were invented
by a hard-working man
who became rich and famous.
His name was Percy Shaw.
   Percy was born in 1890,
in Boothtown, near Halifax, Yorkshire.
There were thirteen children in his family.
Luckily his parents were able to rent
a big old house for 12½p a week.
That sounds very cheap,
but Percy's father only earned £1 a week.

Every day, before going to school,
Percy cleaned fifteen pairs of boots.
Then he fetched the water for the house
from a well and collected vegetables
from the garden.
After school he helped
in his father's home workshop.
Percy enjoyed working with his hands
and using his father's tools.

When Percy was thirteen
he left school, but at first he
could not find a job that he liked.

Percy had several jobs in factories
and one day a factory where he
was working caught fire.

The fire burnt fiercely and
men from the factory
could not put it out.
The fire engine was slow in coming
because it was pulled by horses.
People watching the fire were worried.

"The gas pipe will blow up,"
they shouted.
"If the fire engine doesn't come soon,
the pipe will explode!"
Still the fire engine did not come.

Percy did not just stand and watch.
He ran up the hill to the gasworks
and turned off the gas supply
to the whole of Boothtown.
So there was no explosion.

For his quick thinking,
Percy was given a reward of 37½p.
You may think that was mean
but Percy did not grumble.
He decided to spend the money wisely
on tools for his father's workshop.

Soon afterwards, Percy's father
lost his job, so Percy went
to help him start a business.
They repaired motor cars.

The business was a great success
and they began to make money.
When old Mr Shaw died,
Percy became his own boss.

In 1930, when Percy was forty,
he started a new business,
building small roads and paths.
To make the work easier
he invented a road-roller,
made from old car parts and lorry wheels.
Percy and his workers
became expert at covering
roads with tar and asphalt.

One night, very late, Percy set out
to drive home from his work.
It was dark and very foggy.
The fog was so thick that he
could hardly see the edge of the road.
Suddenly he came to a bad bend.
The road was high on a hill.
On his right was a long drop
down over a cliff.
Percy knew that if he did not follow
the road he would crash over the cliff.
He was scared.

Just then he saw two pinpoints
of bright light on his right.
They were the eyes of a cat
which was sitting on a fence.
The cat's eyes worked like mirrors.
They reflected the light
from the car head lamps.

Percy saw them just in time.
He knew that the cat must be sitting
near the top of the cliff.
For a moment Percy was terrified,
but he kept calm.
Steering the car sharply left,
he just missed the cliff edge.

What a lucky escape!
The cat had saved Percy's life
— or rather, its eyes had.
Percy never forgot that foggy night.
That was when he got the idea
for the catseyes.
He imagined a line of reflectors
along the middle
of all the main roads.
They would make driving safe
because it would be easy
to follow a winding road.

His idea was so new then,
that even his friends laughed.
"Don't waste your time
and money," they told him.

Percy took no notice.
He had saved some money
from the road-making business.
He decided to use this money
to work on his wonderful idea.

Percy tried to make something
that would work like a cat's eyes.
First he tried using marbles
stuck in clay.
But he needed to get very strong
clear glass to make the marbles.
To find the right sort of glass
he travelled two thousand kilometres
to a glass-making factory
in Eastern Europe.

His next problem was to slant
the glass "eyes" to make them reflect
car lights so that a driver
could see them easily in the dark.
After much trying out and testing,
Percy found out how to fix
the eyes into rubber pads.
Then he made an iron frame, to go
just below the top of the road.
When cars ran over them,
the glass catseyes would be pushed
down inside the frame,
without getting broken.

    Percy had another clever idea,
almost the cleverest part
of the invention.
Inside the iron frame
Percy put more rubber pads.
Then, when the catseyes were pushed
into the frame, they were wiped
by the rubber pads.
The pads were like eyelids,
keeping the catseyes clean.

Now it was time to test
the catseyes on real roads,
to see if they worked properly.
Percy did this in a very cheeky way.
He pretended to be a road repair man.
At night his men dug up roads
in Halifax and Bradford.
Then they planted the catseyes
in the middle of the road.
After doing this, Percy
and his men watched carefully.

Did the catseyes reflect
the light properly?
Did they help drivers to stay
on the left side of the road?
They worked very well indeed.
Percy was delighted.
He knew that his idea worked.

That was in 1934.
Percy hoped to sell
thousands of his catseyes.
But they were so unusual
that nobody wanted to buy them.
Nobody was really interested
until the Second World War started.

Then, in 1939, enemy bombers
started to attack Britain by night.
It was dangerous to show any lights at all.
Cars had to use dim lighting.
This made night driving unsafe.
So catseyes were fitted in the roads.
They reflected even dim lights
so driving at night was made safe.
Catseyes did not reflect light
up into the sky,
so bomber pilots did not see them.

Today millions of catseyes
are in use, making night driving
safe all over the world.

●　　●　　●　　●　　●　　●

When he died in 1975, aged 85,
Percy Shaw was a rich man.
He enjoyed working hard all his life.
He enjoyed resting too.
Percy liked smoking his pipe,
playing golf, and driving
his gleaming Rolls Royce.
In the evenings, he liked to watch
his three big television sets,
each switched on to a different channel.

Spotlight on a Shady Wall

Chalk a long looped and wavy line
all along a big wall.
The wall must be in the shade.
Do this on a sunny day.

Use a mirror to reflect the sun
on to the wall.
It will make a bright spot of light.

Can you follow the chalked line
with the spot of light?
Can friends do it faster?

Sonar

Did you know that ships have
special machines to tell them
how far away things are under the water?
These machines are called sonars.
The captain of the ship looks
at the sonar machine.
On a dial like a television screen
he can see patches of light.
These tell him how far away
underwater things are,
such as a shoal of fish,
a submarine or the sea-bed.

The word SONAR is made up of
the first letters of these words:
*So*und *N*avigation *A*nd *R*anging.
What do these words mean?
Navigation is the way the captain
guides a ship along its course.
Ranging means finding the range,
that is, finding how far away
something is.

This is how sonar works.
It uses very short bursts of
very high-pitched sound.
These sounds are too high
for human ears to hear,
just as a dog-whistle gives out sound
too high for us to hear.
Sonar sound is much, much higher
than the highest note a singer can reach.

A sonar machine sends
these very high-pitched sounds
through the sea water.
When the sounds meet something
like a submarine or a shoal of fish,
the sound bounces back as an echo.

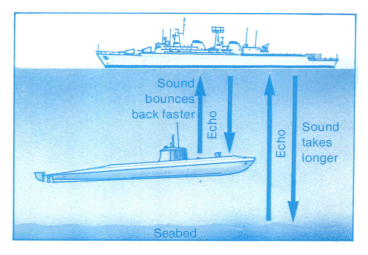

The sonar machine picks up these echoes.
It measures how long the sound takes
to go from the ship to the submarine
and back again.   From this it works out
how far away the submarine is.
From the shape on the dial of the machine
the captain can usually tell whether
he is near a submarine or a shoal of fish.

   You can do a little test on echoes
like this.   Go into the playground
and stand near the wall of a tall building.
It is best to do this
when there is not too much noise.
Stand thirty metres away from the wall.

Now clap your hands once, hard.
You should be able to hear
the echo of your clap a moment later.
Now stand further away from the wall
and clap your hands again.
You should hear the echo
after a little longer time.
This is because sound takes time
to go from your hands to the wall and back.

You can see how long sound can take
to reach you when you watch men
banging in posts from far away.

It takes quite a time
for the sound to reach you.
If the men are a long way away,
you see the post being hit
but you do not hear the sound of it
for another second.

•   •   •   •   •   •

Sound travels through water
even better than it does through air.
That is why sonar machines
work so well under water.

Animals in the sea have their own kind
of sonar.   Dolphins and porpoises
make "boops" of sound under water.
Then they listen for the echoes
that come back to them.
These echoes tell them
where there is a shoal of fish
that they can hunt.

Or the echoes may tell them that
there is a dangerous shark near by.
Then they swim away as quickly as they can.

Some flying animals also use sonar.
Bats have a very high-pitched squeak
which is their kind of sonar.

The squeaks bounce off walls or
the branches of trees.   In that way,
bats can tell how far they are
from the walls or branches.
This is how bats find their way
in the dark, even though they fly very fast.

Many people believe that bats are blind,
but this is not true.
They can see in the daylight
but they cannot see in the dark.
They use their squeak sonar instead.

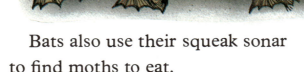

Bats also use their squeak sonar
to find moths to eat.
The bat's ears are sharp enough
to hear the tiny echoes from the soft moth.
But the moths have found a way
to escape from the bats.
When they hear the bats
they drop to the ground and lie "doggo".

They pretend that they are dead.
Then the bat cannot find them.

You can test this for yourself
on a warm summer evening
when there are moths flying about.

Wet your finger,
then wipe it round the rim
of a wine glass.

The glass gives out a steady, high-pitched note.
It also gives out higher notes
that you cannot hear.
These very high notes
are like the bat's sonar squeak.
When the moths hear this note
they think it is a bat near by.
They drop to the ground and
pretend they are dead.
But they are not dead.
You will see them fly off again
after a little while.

Mrs Graham's Balloon Adventure

This adventure happened
more than a hundred years ago.
It was 10 o'clock
on a wet August evening in 1850
and the people of London were waiting
to see a balloon take off.
It was raining hard
and the people carried umbrellas
or wore heavy raincoats.

They were waiting in the rain
for a brave lady called Mrs Graham.
She was going to go up over London
in her huge, black and yellow striped
balloon.   The balloon was filled with
a gas made from coal
and this made it lighter than air.

As soon as Mrs Graham was ready,
the men holding the ropes would let go.
Then the balloon would float into the sky.
Mrs Graham would go with it,

in a little basket
hanging underneath the balloon.

But Mrs Graham was not ready.
She was worried by the rain.
The rope netting over the balloon
and the basket underneath it
were soaking wet.
This made them much heavier and
Mrs Graham was worried that the balloon
would not lift the extra weight.
She was afraid that she would
have to tell the people
that the flight would not take place.

Then the rain stopped.
Mrs Graham decided to take a risk.
She climbed inside the wet basket.
The crowd cheered.

"Hurrah!" they shouted.
"Hurrah for Mrs Graham."
The people cheered and a brass band
played a merry tune.
Then Mrs Graham's men
undid the ropes holding the balloon.

"Let go!" shouted Mrs Graham.
The balloon shot up into the air.
It only just missed some trees
and the crowd let out a cry.
They were worried about her now.
But Mrs Graham waved down to the people.
She was all right.

Then she threw out some sand.
This made the balloon lighter
and it rose higher into the air.

By now the balloon was several hundred
metres above the ground.
The people below looked smaller and smaller
as the balloon rose into the darkness.
The noise of their cheering
became fainter and fainter,
and the balloon floated alone
in the black, starless night.

It was very quiet.
There was no whistle of wind
in the ropes and netting
because now the balloon was drifting
along with the wind.
Mrs Graham could see the lights
of London below, but she could hear nothing.
Then the balloon floated up into a cloud.
The lights disappeared and
Mrs Graham could see nothing at all.
Inside the cloud it was damp and cold.
It was like being inside a thick fog.

The balloon was still rising and
it was becoming colder.
Mrs Graham shivered and
wrapped her coat around herself.
At last the balloon rose
above the clouds.
Moonlight lit up the basket
and the great balloon above.
The clear sky was filled with stars
and the clouds shone like snowfields.
Mrs Graham shivered again.

"I must start to go down,"
she said to herself.
She pulled a string fixed to a valve
on top of the balloon.
This let some gas escape from the balloon.
Slowly the balloon began to drop.
Because there was less gas,
the weight of the ropes and the basket
were pulling it down towards
the ground.   The balloon sank
through the clouds
into the dark world beneath.

It was still very quiet,
but when Mrs Graham looked down
she could see smoke and sparks.
There was a train down there.
The sparks were coming from its funnel.
Now she could hear the hooting
of the engine.

Mrs Graham pulled the valve string again.
Gas hissed out from the balloon
and it began to drop faster.
She was close to the ground now
and could see the trees below her.
They looked like black ghosts.

The balloon swept over the fields
and Mrs Graham let down a long rope
with an iron hook on the end.
There was a sudden jerk.
The hook was caught in a ditch.
Now the balloon could not
sail with the wind
and it began to tilt over.
Mrs Graham was afraid
but she knew what to do.

She had to let the gas out of the balloon.
She pulled the valve string again and again.
Bang!   The basket hit the ground.
Mrs Graham fell out on to the wet grass.
  As the basket rolled over,
Mrs Graham kept pulling the valve string.
For half an hour she fought the wind
which rolled the balloon about her.
Then, when the wind was quieter,
she heard a voice.   There was a light too.
It was a policeman with an oil-lamp.
He ran towards her to help
with the bumping basket.
  "Keep the light away,"
shouted Mrs Graham.
"The balloon is filled with coal-gas.
It will explode if that light
comes too near."
The policeman put down his lamp
and ran on to help her.
  Together they held the balloon.
Together they let the gas out.
But it was a big balloon to empty

and before they had finished
another man appeared.
He too had an oil-lamp
and he brought it too close.
With a flash of yellow flame
the gas caught fire.

The balloon was destroyed
and Mrs Graham's face and hands
were badly burnt.
Her flight had ended badly
but this did not stop Mrs Graham.
Less than a month later
she was bravely flying a balloon again.

Hot-Air Balloons

Mrs Graham's balloon was filled with
coal-gas.   Coal-gas is lighter than air,
so the balloon rose up easily.

Another way of making a balloon rise
is to fill it with hot air.   As long as the
air is kept hot the balloon will stay up.

This kind of balloon is open at the foot
and the air inside is heated by a burner
which hangs underneath the open end.
When the burner is turned on, the air
gets hot and the balloon rises.
When the burner is turned off, the air cools
and the balloon starts to come down.

Hot air balloons travel with the wind
and they can go great distances.
A balloon called *Sultan* holds the
long-distance record.   In 1980 it travelled
a distance of almost 675 kilometres in
Western Australia.

The greatest height ever reached
by a hot-air balloon is 17 400 metres.
This balloon was called *Innovation*.

Stones that Fall from the Sky

On the 13th of September 1768,
some farm workers
were busy in a field in France,
when they heard a sound like thunder.
Then there was a low whistle,
and something fell through the air
and landed in the grass.
They ran to the spot.

There they found a burning hot stone
as big as a large bun.
It was half buried in the ground.
The men took the stone to the nearest town.
"This stone fell from the sky," they said.
A famous scientist called Lavoisier
studied the stone.
He said that the men must be wrong.
"Stones do not fall from the sky,"
he told them.
"You saw a stone struck by lightning."
The men were very upset.
They knew that the stone had come
from the sky.   They had seen it land.

●   ●   ●   ●   ●   ●

Now we know that the men were right.
Stones do sometimes fall from the sky.
These stones are called meteorites.
They fall to the earth from space.
They may be pieces of a planet
or a moon that blew up long, long ago.
Nobody is really sure.

You may have seen a meteorite
falling through the night sky.
It travels so fast that it starts to burn
when it hits the air around the earth.
    Most meteorites are no bigger
than grains of sand or peas.
Nearly all of them burn
before they can land.
They turn to dust in the air.
Only the bigger ones reach the ground.
About a hundred and fifty meteorites
reach the ground every year.

Most of them are quite small and there is
only one known case of a meteorite
hitting a man.

Once in a very long while
the earth is struck
by a giant meteorite.
Scientists think that the Barringer Crater
in the American state of Arizona
was made by a meteorite as big as a house.
It exploded, leaving a crater
more than one hundred and fifty metres deep
and more than one kilometre wide.

Mr Harting and the Snails

Late one dark and stormy night
Mr Harting was working in his room
when he heard a strange noise.
He could hear the wind and rain outside,
but there was another sound.
It was like sweet music far away.
What could it be?
    Some months later he heard
the strange music again.
This time the curtains were open
and Mr Harting could see the glass.
A snail was creeping across the window.
The snail was making the music
by rubbing the glass as it crept along.

You can do the same thing
with a wine glass.
You rub it round the top
with a clean, wet finger.
Your wet finger stops and slips
many times each second,
jerking the glass to and fro very quickly.
This makes the glass sing.

Mr Harting told his friend Bobby Jones
about the musical snail.

"Snails sound interesting," said Bobby.
"Can I keep them as pets?" he asked.

"Yes, but you will have to make
a snailery," replied Mr Harting.
"Find a big glass jar and
put some damp earth inside.
The snails can live in there."

"How do I feed the snails?"
Bobby wanted to know.

"You give them oats and
crushed chalk," replied Mr Harting.
"The snails eat the chalk,
and the lime in it

makes their shells strong."

"What about lettuce?" asked Bobby.
"Can they eat lettuce?"

"Yes," said Mr Harting, "they can,
but it makes them leave messy droppings."

Bobby found a large glass jar
and made his snailery.
Then he put in two garden snails.
Once a week he tipped out the dirt
and put in fresh earth.
He kept the earth damp
by sprinkling a little water on it
every day.

Both snails laid eggs in holes they dug.
Bobby took the eggs out and put them
in some earth in another jar.
The eggs looked like pearls.

●　　●　　●　　●　　●　　●

Bobby's sister Mandy did not like
the snails.　　She thought they were pests.
Mr Harting agreed.
During the spring and summer,
snails ate the vegetables in his garden.
They particularly liked strawberries
and cabbages.
　　"What do they do in winter?" asked Bobby.
　　"They go to sleep," said Mr Harting.
"They sleep right through the cold weather
and only wake up when
the warmer weather comes.
Did you know," he added,
"that some kinds of snails can sleep
for three or four years?　　They don't eat
and they don't drink during all that time.
One snail that was supposed to be dead

woke up in a museum.   It had been
inside a glass case for several years.
People were amazed."

Bobby asked if it was true
that people could eat snails.

"Yes," said Mr Harting.
"Last year I had lunch
at The Miner's Arms, in Somerset.
There were snails on the menu
so I tried some."

"What did they taste like?" asked Mandy.

"A bit fishy," said Mr Harting,
"but they were nicely cooked
in Somerset cider and tasty herbs."

• • • • • •

After thirty days, Bobby's snails' eggs
hatched.   The babies were perfect,
with paper-thin shells.
Bobby was so pleased
that he asked Mandy a riddle.

"What animal walks on one foot?"
he asked.   Mandy knew the answer.

"A snail," she said.
Mr Harting put a snail on
a sheet of glass.
Then he held the glass upside down,
so that they could see the snail's foot.
  "Look," he said, "the snail's foot
seems to suck its way along."
The children watched as the sucking foot
pulled the little animal forward.
  Mr Harting asked the children
if they had ever seen snail tracks
shining in the sunlight.
A snail makes a road of slime,
called mucus.   Mucus comes
from a place under the snail's mouth.

It stops the animal getting hurt
by sharp things.
A snail can slide over
the edge of a razor blade,
without getting cut.

Mandy began to like snails.
She watched the babies growing up
and saw the way they changed.
She asked why snails had horns.

"The bottom ones are for smelling,"
replied Mr Harting.
"The top ones have eyes on their tips.
Try to touch them with a finger."
Mandy did it very gently,
but before she could touch,
the snail pulled its eyes in.

Mandy smiled and said,
    "It's like pulling in
the fingers of a glove."

●   ●   ●   ●   ●   ●

One day when they were feeding
the baby snails, Mandy asked,
    "How do snails eat?   Do they have teeth?"
Mr Harting laughed.
    "A snail's dentist would have a hard time.
Garden snails have twenty-five thousand
tiny teeth, like a file.
When snails eat,
the file rips the food to bits.
They can even gnaw limestone.
That's how they eat the little bits
of crushed chalk that we give them.
Can you remember why they need
the chalk, Mandy?"
Mandy had not forgotten.
    "For their shells, of course," she said.
    "Snails can even eat their way out
of cardboard boxes," said Mr Harting.

"Sometimes they get into letterboxes
and eat the letters.   When this happens,
the postman has to stick labels
on the envelopes.   They say,
'Damaged by snails'."

•   •   •   •   •   •

Mr Harting thought that
the children were becoming
real snail experts.

   "Why don't you form a Snail-Watching
Club?" he asked.   "You could watch your
baby snails as they grow up.   You could hold
snail races, too.   All you need is
a big board and some garden snails."

   "That would be fun," said Bobby.
"Wouldn't it, Mandy?"

   "And remember," said Mr Harting.
"Watch your snails as much as you can.
You might find out something
about snails that nobody
has seen before.   Then you would
really be snail experts."

How to Hold a Snail Race

Make the race track on a big board
about forty to fifty centimetres square.
Draw a small circle
in the middle of a big one.
You can chalk around
a plate and a big bowl.

Find some garden snails.
(Look in old damp walls.)
Give them names.

Start by putting the snails
inside the small circle.
The winner of the race
is the first snail
to get out of the big circle.

Animal Speeds

Snails travel very slowly
on their one foot.
So if you decide to have a snail race
it will not be finished quickly.
A snail's top speed is about
eight centimetres a minute.

    Some animals, of course, can move
very fast indeed.
The fastest animal in the world
is a bird called the spine-tailed swift.
It can reach a speed of
171 kilometres an hour.

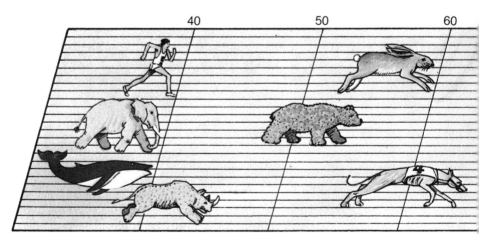

Here are the possible top speeds
for some mammals.

Human being	40 kilometres an hour
Elephant	40
Blue whale	40
Rhinoceros	45
Grizzly bear	55
Rabbit	60
Greyhound	65
Race horse	80
Lion	80
Deer	80
Cheetah	100

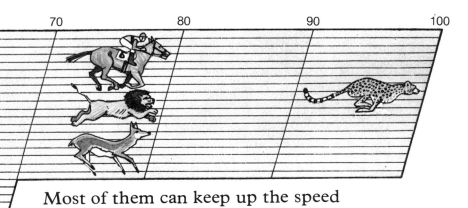

Most of them can keep up the speed
for only a very short time.

The Tiny Worlds
a Dutchman Saw

Do you know what a microscope is?
It makes little things look bigger,
as much as 100 000 times bigger.

If you use one to look at
a drop of blood, you see a watery liquid
filled with tiny red and white blobs.
These blobs are blood cells,
which help to keep us fit and well.
Today, with a modern microscope,
it is easy to see these cells,
but three hundred years ago
it was very difficult.

The first man to see blood cells
with a microscope was a Dutchman.
His name sounds "Lay-ven-hook",
but you spell it Leeuwenhoek.

Leeuwenhoek lived in Holland
three hundred years ago.
He kept a shop in the town of Delft,
where he sold ribbons and cloth.

During the day he did this.
In the evenings he made microscopes.

Leeuwenhoek used a lens at work.
He looked through it to check the cloth
he bought and sold.   He also used this lens
to look at other things — insects, flowers,
finger-prints and pennies.
His lens made them all look
about three times bigger.

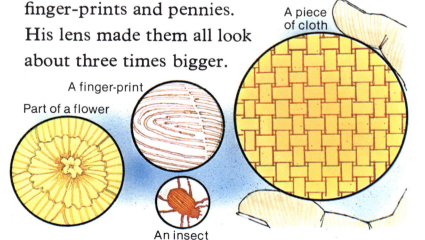

A piece of cloth

A finger-print

Part of a flower

An insect

This was not big enough for Leeuwenhoek,
so he made his own lenses.
The lenses he made were very small,
but they were much more powerful
than the lenses anyone else could make.
He kept the way he did it a secret.

To make a microscope, he put a tiny lens
between two sheets of metal.
It looked like a small bat
with a little round window in it.
The "window" was his lens.
Things he wanted to look at were put on
a thin rod, or pin, behind the lens.

Liquids were put in tubes which he glued
to the rod.

By turning screws, he could make
what he was looking at come clearly
into sight.

He looked at a fly with his microscope.
What a monster it was —
with eyes like black golf-balls.
He could see that each fly's eye
was hundreds of eyes in one.
He must have wanted to know
how the world looked to a fly.

He wanted to know why flies did not
fall off when they walked on the ceiling.
Through his microscope he saw
that a fly's feet had sticky pads and hairs.
That was why it could walk upside-down.

His microscopes helped him to find out
about the life story of the tiny flea.
He saw how powerful its back legs were.
They helped it to jump as high as
nineteen and a half centimetres.
This is one hundred and thirty times
its own height.

Fleas bite other animals and make them itch.
How Leeuwenhoek laughed when he found
even smaller animals, called mites,
biting fleas!

Leeuwenhoek made special microscopes
to watch the way the blood flowed
in a bat's wing, in a rabbit's ear
and in a tadpole's tail.

One day he took some water from a lake.
In summer the water was cloudy,

but in winter it was clear.
People said that summer weather
made the lake cloudy,
but Leeuwenhoek was not so sure.

When he looked at a drop of
the lake water in a microscope,
he could not believe his eyes.
The drop was alive with hundreds
of tiny swimming monsters.
Some looked like living slippers.
Some were like balls made of lace.
Others lashed whip-like tails.
None of them was more than
one millimetre across.
Leeuwenhoek had found a whole world
in a drop of water.

He wrote letters to scientists
about his work.   In his letters
he mixed town gossip with news about
the strange things he was seeing
with his microscope.

Some scientists found it hard
to use his microscopes.

They could not see the little animals.
Their eyesight was not sharp enough,
so they said that he told lies.
But, after a time,
they too saw the little animals.
They had to admit that he was
a great scientist.

One of Leeuwenhoek's ideas was to scrape
his teeth and mix the scum with water.
Looking at the scum with a microscope,
he saw what, today, we would call germs.
He discovered that the germs were killed
when he drank hot coffee,
but he never had any idea that germs
might make people ill.

When he died, aged 91, Leeuwenhoek
was famous.   His name was known
all over Europe, but there were mysteries
about his work in science.
Nobody ever saw his best microscopes.
In fact nobody was able to make
such good lenses as Leeuwenhoek did
for the next hundred years.

Using a Water-Drop Lens

Find a clean plastic bag
and cut a piece from it.
It must be the kind of bag
you can see through.
Dip a clean finger
into clean water in a cup.
Use your finger to put
a small round drop of water
on to the piece of plastic.
Put the plastic on a piece of
clear glass.
Now you have
a water-drop microscope.

   Use it to look at
a piece of cloth,
a postage stamp,
newspaper printing,
and anything else
you like.

A Feast of Colours

Would you eat eggs
if they were blue?

• • • • • •

One day a scientist had a party
for his scientist friends.
The party was a test
to see how important
colours were in food.
He lit the room in clever ways,
to give the food different colours.
　　Fresh peas looked black as coal.
Meat seemed to be grey.
Celery was bright pink.
The milk looked like blood.
Salad was sky-blue.
Lemons were orange.
The coffee was sickly yellow.
Even the nuts seemed to be scarlet.
　　Would you have eaten the meal
— even if you were hungry?

Most people at the party ate very little.
The few people who did eat much
became ill.
Yet the food was good,
well-cooked and tasty.

Only one man ate all his dinner
without getting ill.
He was a blind man.

Do you think that
the colours of food are important?

The Voyage of the Beagle

In December 1831, a sailing ship
left Plymouth, England,
to sail round the world.
The ship was called the *Beagle*.
It was only 28 metres long
and carried 74 people.
Among them was a young man
called Charles Darwin.

Darwin was there as a naturalist.
His job was to study
the plants and animals
he found during the *Beagle*'s long journey.

•　　•　　•　　•　　•　　•

This story tells of the *Beagle*'s visit
to some islands in the Pacific Ocean.
The Galapagos Islands are about
a thousand kilometres from Ecuador,
a country in South America.

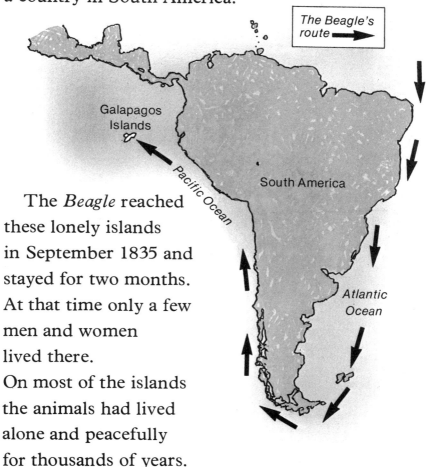

The *Beagle* reached
these lonely islands
in September 1835 and
stayed for two months.
At that time only a few
men and women
lived there.
On most of the islands
the animals had lived
alone and peacefully
for thousands of years.

103

When the sailors landed they found
huge turtles and tortoises
and strange lizards
that looked like dragons.

Darwin had a bumpy and very slow ride
on the back of one of the tortoises.
In ten minutes his tortoise moved
only fifty metres!
  The animals were not afraid of people
so Darwin was able to study them very closely.

He discovered something very interesting.
He discovered that the animals
on the Galapagos Islands
were not quite like the animals
that he had seen in South America.
For instance, in some ways the lizards
that looked like dragons
were similar to the lizards
that Darwin had seen in South America.
But in other ways they were very different.
It was the same with the many different
types of finches on the islands.
They were different from the finches
that Darwin had seen in South America.

   Even more important to Darwin
was his discovery
that the animals on one island
were not quite like those on another.
A tortoise or a finch
on one island was not quite like
a tortoise or a finch on another island.
So by looking at the shell of a tortoise
or the beak of a finch

he could tell which island it had
come from.   All the finches
had dull-coloured feathers and short tails.
All of them laid four pink and white eggs
in nests with little roofs.
But they all had different beaks.
On one island they had strong thick beaks
for cracking open nuts and seeds.

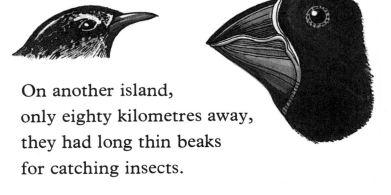

On another island,
only eighty kilometres away,
they had long thin beaks
for catching insects.

•   •   •   •   •   •

Now Darwin had many puzzles to solve.
He knew that the animals of the Galapagos
Islands had come from South America
thousands and thousands of years ago.
Darwin wanted to know
how they had got to the islands.

He asked the same question
about the plants and seeds
that the animals and birds ate.
How had they got from South America?
Finally he wanted to know why the animals
were different on each island.

The answers to these questions
did not come quickly.
Darwin thought about them
for the rest of his life,
and he gave different answers
at different times.

First Darwin thought about the birds.
He decided that they had flown from
South America and landed on
the Galapagos Islands.
Some landed on one island, some
on another.   On each island
they ate the food that they could find.
On some islands there were more seeds
and so the finches ate them.
On others there were more insects
and there the finches ate insects.

    Gradually the finches
on the different islands changed.
It took thousands of years,
but slowly they changed to suit the food
they could find on each island.
That was why some finches had
short strong beaks to crack open seeds,
and other finches had long thin beaks
for catching insects.

    Then Darwin wanted to know where
the food that the birds ate came from.
How had the seeds of the first plants
reached the island?
Darwin decided that the seeds had floated
across the sea from Ecuador.

There is a sea current that moves out
from Ecuador to the islands.
This sea current could have swept the seeds
out to the islands.   It moves
at about thirty-five kilometres per day
so it would take over a month
for seeds to get from Ecuador
to the Galapagos Islands.
    Could they live that long
in cold salt water?
    Some scientists were sure that they
could not.   They said that the seeds
would never grow into plants
after being so long in sea water.
Darwin made a test to see whether
they were right.
He put seeds in cold salt water.
He found that they could stand
being in salt water for over four months
and still grow into plants.
Now he knew that the seeds could easily
float from Ecuador to the islands
and grow there.

Darwin found another thing on the islands
that puzzled him.
When the tide went out
it left pools of sea water among the rocks.
This water was very salty,
but in the pools Darwin found
the shells of animals
that live in fresh water.
How could they have got there?
He knew that they could not have floated
across from Ecuador because these animals
cannot live in salt water.

Darwin puzzled about this for many years.
It nearly drove him mad, he said.
Then one day he saw some ducks
walking out of a country pond in England.
Round their feet were strands
of duck weed and in the duck weed
were freshwater shells!
At last he saw how the shells
could have reached the islands.
They could have been carried by ducks
flying from Ecuador to the islands.

Darwin worked out that the ducks
took about sixteen hours to fly
to the islands and he made a test to see
how long the shells could live
out of water.   He found that
some freshwater shells could live
up to twenty hours out of water.
Now he was fairly sure of the answer.
The ducks had carried the shells
in weed caught round their legs.

●   ●   ●   ●   ●   ●

It was tests like these
that made Darwin sure of his ideas.
He asked many other questions
about the way in which
animals and plants live and he
answered them all in the same way.
He watched and thought
and then did tests to see
whether his ideas were right.
That is the way in which you can be
a scientist.

Alexander Fleming

Alexander Fleming was a great doctor
and a very lucky man.
He discovered a drug that has saved
thousands of lives.
This drug is called penicillin
and it is often used by doctors today.
Sore throats, boils and blood poisoning
are just a few of the diseases
that penicillin helps to cure.

Alexander Fleming discovered penicillin
by a stroke of luck.   But this piece of luck
was not the start of the story.

● ● ● ● ● ●

Alexander Fleming was born on
the 6th of August 1881, on a farm in Scotland.
He grew up there and when he was a boy
he liked to look for birds' nests.

He was also very good at tickling trout.
This is a way of catching these fish
in your hands.

You have to put your hand
in a trout stream and hold it there
quite still.
When a trout swims on to your hand
you close it swiftly and smoothly
and pull the trout out of the water.
You must be patient
and then very swift and sure.

  When Alexander Fleming grew up
and became a doctor,
he found that these hobbies
were useful to him.
Tickling for trout had taught him
how to use his hands skilfully.

Birds' nesting had taught him
how to look carefully and think about
what he saw.

Alexander had always wanted to be a doctor,
but when he left school
at the age of fifteen
he had to go to work in an office.
For five years he worked there.
Then, when he was twenty
he was left some money.
He left the office
and went to St Mary's Hospital
in London.
There he studied to become a doctor.

Fleming became a doctor
the day before his twenty-fifth birthday.
He stayed at St Mary's Hospital
and worked there with another doctor.
He helped with experiments
and he studied the sick people
in the hospital.   By doing this
Fleming learnt a lot about disease
and how the human body fights it.

He decided then that
he wanted to spend his life
finding out more about disease.
Most of all he wanted to know
how the body fights disease.
It was tiring work,
for he had to keep long hours.
It was also dangerous,
because he could have caught diseases
from the sick people he saw
in the hospital.

For eight years he worked in the hospital.
Then came the First World War.
Britain and France went to war
with Germany.   Doctors were needed
to help on the battlefields
and Fleming went to France.
He worked there in a hospital
for wounded soldiers.

Most of the soldiers had wounds
caused by bullets or shells.
These wounds are very difficult to clean
because they are so ragged and torn.

The bones and skin are smashed to pieces
by the explosives.
The doctors tried to clean these wounds
with iodine, but this did not work.
It did not kill the germs
which caused blood poisoning.
Hundreds and thousands of soldiers
died from blood poisoning,
which they caught because their wounds
were not clean.

Fleming was sure that there were better ways
to clean wounds and prevent blood poisoning.

He started experiments to find them.
He took some blood
from a soldier with blood poisoning.
He put half this blood
into a test tube with some iodine.
He put the other half of the blood
into another test tube on its own.
Then he watched both test tubes very carefully.
He watched to see
what happened to the germs in the blood.
Did the iodine kill them?
That was what Fleming wanted to know.
Soon he knew the answer.
Iodine did not kill these germs.
Instead, more and more germs
grew in the blood with iodine in it.

   Then Fleming looked at the blood
with no iodine in it.
This was different.
There were fewer germs in this blood.
It was fighting the germs on its own,
while the blood with iodine in it
did not fight germs.

Why did this happen?
Fleming could not find out immediately.
But he had learnt that iodine
did not help the body to fight germs.
Now he had to look for a drug
that could do this.
He had to find a wonder drug.
It was not easy.

First of all,
Fleming had to grow germs.
He grew them carefully
on little glass dishes
called Petri dishes.

Then he tried to kill these germs
with drugs.   He experimented
with many different drugs
but he could not find one that
would kill the germs he had grown.

Then one day he found
that tears kill some germs.
To make himself cry,
Fleming took small slices of lemon
and put them in his eyes.

This hurt a lot.
But it made his eyes water, and
this was what Fleming wanted.
A single drop of his tears
killed the cold germs
that he had grown in a glass dish.

This was a beginning,
but it did not lead to his wonder drug.
He made more and more experiments,
always looking for a drug
that would kill germs
but would not harm the body.

He did not find it for twenty years —
and then he found it by luck.

Fleming was working again
in St Mary's Hospital.
It was a sunny day
and the windows were open.
Near by were some glass dishes
in which Fleming was growing germs.
He noticed that a mould
was growing in the dishes.
It had blown in with the wind.
The dishes were spoiled,

but Fleming did not throw them away.
Instead he looked more closely at the dishes
and saw that some of the germs had gone.
This mould was a germ killer.
Fleming had found his wonder drug.
It killed germs,
but it did not harm the body.
He called it penicillin,
because that is the Latin name
for the mould he had found.

Penicillin was a very strong drug,
but it was difficult to make.
Fleming found that he could not use it
in the hospital, so he had to look
for other germ killers.

No one thought any more about penicillin
for thirteen years.   Then two scientists
began working on tear drops.   They read
what Fleming had written about tears.
They also read what he had written
about his discovery of penicillin.
Like Fleming they tried to make penicillin.
Unlike him they succeeded.

In 1941 they tried out penicillin
on a policeman.
He was dying of blood poisoning.
The doctors said he could not live,
so the scientists decided
to try the penicillin that they had made.
It was kill or cure!
They gave him penicillin every three hours.
The next day he was much better.
He even wanted to eat.
Then the penicillin ran out.
There was no more of it left.
A month later the policeman died.
He would have lived
if there had been enough penicillin.

The two scientists made more of the drug,
and tried it on other sick people.
It worked perfectly —
all of them were cured.

●　　●　　●　　●　　●　　●

Penicillin was the strongest germ killer
that doctors knew.

During the Second World War
very few soldiers died of blood poisoning.
Penicillin saved thousands of lives.

Fleming and the two scientists
who had made the penicillin
were given the Nobel prize.
This is the highest prize in medicine.
They deserved the prize,
because their work
had made life safer for everybody.

Grow Your Own Moulds

What you need:

Six empty jars

A lid for each jar

Sticky tape

20 grams of each of these things:

 cheese

bread

used tea leaves

What you do:

1 Put half the cheese in one jar. Put the other half in another jar.

2 Do the same with the bread and the tea leaves.

3 Put a lid on each jar.

4 Put sticky tape round the lids.

5 Put a label on each jar.

6 Find a warm, dark place–a cupboard or drawer.

7 Put a jar of cheese, a jar of bread and a jar of tea leaves into your warm, dark place. Leave them there for a week. Take them out when they have gone mouldy.

8 Put the other three jars in the coldest place you can find. Take them out at the same time.

9 Make a table like this to show what happened.

	Warm place	Cold place
Cheese		
Bread		
Tea leaves		

Tick to show which things grew mould.

10 What does your table show?

Note to teacher:
Do not open any of the jars after they have been sealed.
Dispose of the jars safely.

Index